Uffizi

The Great Masterpieces

SCALA

The Galleria degli Uffizi and Its Collections

The Uffizi, one of the oldest and most important museums in the world, was not originally intended to house works of art. In 1560 the painter, architect and writer Giorgio Vasari (1511-74) was commissioned by Cosimo I de' Medici (1519-74) to design a large building adjoining Palazzo Vecchio as a suitable seat for the city's magistracies, in other words the *uffizi* or "offices" for the administrative and judicial system of the increasingly powerful duchy of Tuscany. To this extraordinary construction with its characteristic U-shaped plan was added, only five years later, an unusual and daring elevated extension that ran across the embankment of the Arno and the Ponte Vecchio, linking it with Palazzo Pitti. Completed in just five months, the Corridoio Vasariano, as it was called, physically and symbolically unified the two centers of power, Palazzo Vecchio, seat of political life, and Palazzo Pitti, residence of the ruling family, in an uninterrupted architectural and urbanistic route that permitted the duke and his court to move between them in complete safety.

It was not until some years later, however, that the real history of the Uffizi as a museum commenced. In 1581 the building had been completed by Bernardo Buontalenti (1531-1608) and the cultured and refined Grand Duke Francesco I, at a time when the Medici dynasty was at the height of its glory, started to move the family's collections of art, made up of ancient and contemporary sculptures, paintings and other

precious objects, to the second floor of the palace. At the same time he gave orders for numerous works of enlargement and embellishment of the building. It was he who was responsible, for instance, for the sumptuous decoration of the corridors with grotesques, commissioned from a group of artists led by Alessandro Allori (1535-1607), and the construction, again to a design by Buontalenti, of the Teatro Mediceo and the Tribuna. The latter is unquestionably the most unusual and famous

part of the gallery, a reflection of the grand duke's eclectic tastes and wide range of cultural interests: octagonal in shape and roofed with a dome terminating in a lantern, it was conceived, in accordance with a complex cosmological symbology, as a sort of sacred temple of the arts in which to put the most important and extraordinary pieces in the collection on show. From that time on the Uffizi, thanks largely to the passion for collecting displayed by the Medici, and by the Lorraine after them, has been continually enriched with magnificent works of art. It is particularly worth mentioning the contributions made by Grand Duke Ferdinando II (1610-70) who, through the inheritance of his wife Vittoria della Rovere, brought a number of extremely important works into the gallery, and by his brother Cardinal Leopoldo (1617-75), whose substantial personal collection entered the Uffizi on his death. Nor should we forget the part played by Anna Maria Luisa, last of the Medici, when she entrusted the family's entire collection of art to the Lorraine in 1737, thereby ensuring its inalienability and that it would remain in the city of Florence forever.

The Galleria degli Uffizi, as we know it today (and as it is presented in this volume), is above all a great picture gallery whose main collection comprises the highest achievements of one of the most extraordinary moments in the entire history of art: the Italian and in particular the Florentine Renaissance. But while the collection of paintings extends well beyond these limits, including Italian and foreign works covering a period stretching from the 13th century to the 18th century, it must also be pointed out that the museum, as a consequence of its origins and history, contains other collections of enormous historical and artistic importance. These include ancient sculpture, one of the largest collections of drawings and prints in the world, a group of tapestries and finally the highly unusual collection of self-portraits, which is still being enlarged today with works by contemporary artists.

Top left, Agnolo Bronzino (Florence 1503-72), *Portrait of Cosimo I in Armor.*

Left, the Uffizi from the Arno and a view of the first corridor.

Right, *Boy Removing a Thorn from His Foot,* Roman copy of a Hellenistic original.

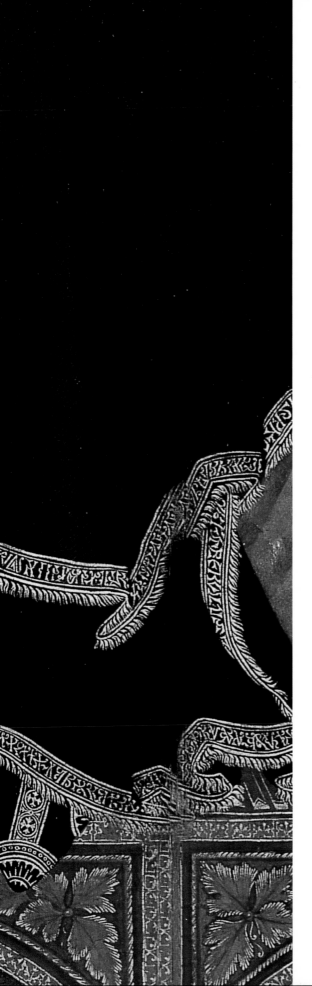

Our exploration of the masterpieces in the Galleria degli Uffizi begins with a series of important examples of early Tuscan painting, culminating in the three great *Maestà* of Cimabue, Duccio and Giotto. Coming from the Florentine churches of Santa Trinita, Santa Maria Novella and Ognissanti respectively, the three large panels, recently restored, represent a crucial moment in the development of Italian art. While in Cimabue's work, still closely bound to the Byzantine iconographic tradition, a new sensibility begins to find expression, discernible above all in the Madonna's gesture indicating the Child, in Duccio's *Maestà* the same iconographic scheme admits a new creativity, most clearly apparent in the sinuosity of the Virgin's cloak, the rich coloring and the complexity of the structure of the throne. But it is in Giotto's masterwork that the new vision of reality fully flowers: the elements of the composition are the same, but the space is represented in convincing perspective and above all the figures have been humanized, with the rigid fixity of Byzantine icons left behind for good.

From the severe beauty of the Florentine *Maestà* we move on to the dazzling refinements of Sienese 14th-century painting, commencing with Simone Martini's *Annunciation*. Here, in the elegant figure of the shy Virgin, shrinking away from the angel, he has created one of the most beautiful Madonnas in the history of art. This is followed by several works by the brothers Ambrogio and Pietro Lorenzetti, characterized by great narrative skills and sophisticated coloristic effects.

Finally, among the 14th-century works of the Florentine school, it is worth singling out Giottino's *Pietà*, in which the artist breaks away from the Giottesque tradition to adopt the realistic style and pathos of Lombard painting.

Pisan artist of the late 12th century

Crucifix with Scenes from the Passion
Tempera on panel, 377 x 231 cm

Master of the Bardi Saint Francis
(active between 1240 and 1270)

Crucifix with Scenes from the Passion
Tempera on panel, 247 x 200 cm

Meliore di Jacopo
(documented in
Florence in 1260)
*Christ the Redeemer
and Four Saints*
Tempera on panel,
85 x 210 cm

**Cenni di Pepo,
called Cimabue**
(Florence c. 1240 -
after 1302)
Santa Trinita Madonna
and detail on pages 8-9
Tempera on panel,
425 x 243 cm

Duccio di Buoninsegna
(Siena c. 1260 - 1318)

Rucellai Madonna and detail on pages 4-5
Tempera on panel,
450 x 290 cm

Giotto di Bondone
(Vespignano, Vicchio di Mugello, c. 1267 - Florence 1337)

Ognissanti Madonna
Tempera on panel,
325 x 204 cm

Giotto

Badia Polyptych
Tempera on panel,
91 x 334 cm

Simone Martini
(Siena c. 1284 -
Avignon 1344)
and **Lippo Memmi**
(Siena, documented
1317 - 1347)

Annunciation
Tempera on panel,
265 x 305 cm

previous pages:
Ambrogio Lorenzetti
(Siena 1285 - c. 1348)
*Four Stories from the
Life of Saint Nicholas*
Tempera on panel,
96 x 35 cm
(each panel)

Ambrogio Lorenzetti
*Presentation in the
Temple* and detail
on pages 18-19
Tempera on panel,
257 x 168 cm

Pietro Lorenzetti
(Siena c. 1280 -
1348?)

*Madonna and Child
with Angels*
Tempera on panel,
145 x 122 cm

Pietro Lorenzetti

*Blessed Humilitas
Altarpiece*
Tempera on panel,
128 x 57 cm (central
panel), 45 x 32
(each scene)

Saint Cecilia Master
(active in Florence
1300 - c. 1320)

*Saint Cecilia and Eight
Scenes from her Life*
Tempera on panel,
85 x 181 cm

**Andrea di Cione,
called Orcagna**
(Florence c. 1320 -
1368)
and Jacopo di Cione
(Florence c. 1330 -
1398)

*Saint Matthew and
Scenes from his Life*
Tempera on panel,
291 x 265 cm

Giottino
(Florence c. 1320/30
- post 1369)

Pietà and detail
on following pages
Tempera on panel,
195 x 134 cm

23

The section of 15th-century paintings opens with a number of works still linked to the International Gothic culture. Outstanding among these is the *Adoration of the Magi* by Gentile da Fabriano, a sumptuous composition set in its rich and precious original frame.

We then move on to the great revolution of the early Renaissance, starting with the *Virgin and Child with Saint Anne* by Masolino and Masaccio and continuing with extraordinary paintings by artists like Fra Angelico, Domenico Veneziano, Filippo Lippi, Vecchietta, Alessio Baldovinetti, Filippino Lippi and Antonio and Piero Pollaiuolo. Among the works of this period, special mention should be made of Paolo Uccello's celebrated *Battle of San Romano*, which in 1492 hung in the chamber of Lorenzo the Magnificent along with two more scenes of the same battle, now in London and in Paris, and of the equally famous *Diptych of the Duke and Duchess of Urbino* by Piero della Francesca, originally located in the Ducal Palace of that city and brought to Florence as the inheritance of Vittoria della Rovere, wife of Ferdinando II de' Medici.

Next we come to the group of paintings by Sandro Botticelli, of which the Uffizi possesses a larger number than any other museum, and which certainly represents one of the highpoints of a visit to the gallery. Most celebrated of all, the two large panels of the *Primavera* and *The Birth of Venus*: dense in profound and in part still mysterious allegorical meanings, Botticelli's two masterpieces should be seen in connection with the Neoplatonic culture rich in philosophical and literary references that gravitated around the court of Lorenzo the Magnificent.

A group of works by Flemish artists bears witness to the close commercial and cultural relations that existed between Florence and Flanders in the 15th century. Among them, the *Portinari Triptych* by Hugo van der Goes, a picture that made a great impression on Florentine artists.

Another highlight of the 15th-century section consists of two of Leonardo's masterworks, the *Annunciation* and the *Adoration of the Magi*. He also painted the two angels at bottom left of Andrea Verrocchio's *Baptism of Christ*.

Among the examples of Umbrian painting are several works executed toward the end of the century by Perugino, while the Lombard school is represented in the Uffizi by Andrea Mantegna's masterpieces.

Gentile da Fabriano
(Fabriano c. 1370 -
Rome 1427)

Adoration of the Magi
Tempera on panel,
300 x 282 cm

following pages:
Lorenzo Monaco
(Siena? c. 1370 -
Florence c. 1425)
and **Cosimo Rosselli**
(Florence 1439 - 1507)

Adoration of the Magi
Tempera on panel,
115 x 177 cm

Masolino
(Panicale in Valdarno
1383? - 1440)
and **Masaccio**
(San Giovanni Valdarno
1401 - Rome 1428)

*Madonna and Child
with Saint Anne*
Tempera on panel,
175 x 103 cm

Masaccio

*Madonna and Child
(Madonna
del Solletico)*
Tempera on panel,
24,5 x 18.2 cm

Fra Angelico
(Vicchio di Mugello
c. 1400 - Rome 1455)

*Coronation
of the Virgin*
Tempera on panel,
112 x 114 cm

Domenico Veneziano
(Venice c. 1400 -
Florence 1461)

*Santa Lucia dei
Magnoli Altarpiece*
Tempera on panel,
209 x 216 cm

Paolo Uccello
(Florence 1397 - 1475)

*The Battle
of San Romano*
Tempera on panel,
182 x 323 cm

Filippo Lippi
(Florence c. 1406 -
Spoleto 1469)

*Coronation
of the Virgin*
Tempera on panel,
220 x 287 cm

**Lorenzo di Pietro
called Vecchietta**
(Siena 1410 - 1480)

Madonna and Saints
Tempera on panel,
156 x 230 cm

Filippo Lippi

*Madonna and Child
with Two Angels*, detail
Tempera on panel,
95 x 62 cm

Alessio Baldovinetti
(Florence 1425 - 1499)

Annunciation
Tempera on panel,
167 x 137 cm

Piero della Francesca
(Borgo San Sepolcro
c. 1410/20 - 1492)
*Diptych of the Duke
and Duchess of Urbino*
(front and back)
Tempera on panel,
47 x 33 cm (each panel)

QVE MODVM REBVS TENVIT SECVNDIS ·
CONIVGIS MAGNI DECORATA RERVM ·
·LAVDE GESTARVM VOLITAT PER ORA ·
CVNCTA VIRORVM ·

CLARVS INSIGNI VEHITVR TRIVMPHO ·
QVEM PAREM SVMMIS DVCIBVS PERHENNIS ·
FAMA VIRTVTVM CELEBRAT DECENTER ·
SCEPTRA TENENTEM ·

Antonio Benci
(Florence c. 1431 -
Rome 1498)
and **Piero Benci**
(Florence c. 1443 -
Rome 1496)
**called the Pollaiuolo
brothers**

*Saints James, Vincent
and Eustace*
Tempera on panel,
172 x 179 cm

Antonio Pollaiuolo

Portrait of a Lady
Tempera on panel,
55 x 34 cm

Antonio Pollaiuolo

Hercules and the Hydra
Tempera on panel,
17 x 12 cm

**Sandro Filipepi
called Botticelli**
(Florence 1445 - 1510)
Adoration of the Magi
Tempera on panel,
111 x 134 cm

Sandro Botticelli
*Virgin and Child
with Saints*
Tempera on panel,
170 x 194 cm

Sandro Botticelli
*Portrait of a Man with
the Medal of Cosimo
the Elder*, detail
Tempera on panel,
57.5 x 44 cm

Sandro Botticelli

*Madonna
of the Magnificat*
Tempera on panel,
diam. 118 cm

Sandro Botticelli

*Madonna of the
Pomegranate* and
detail on pages 50-51
Tempera on panel,
diam. 143.5 cm

Sandro Botticelli

La Primavera (*Spring*)
and detail on pages
54-55
Tempera on panel,
203 x 314 cm

Sandro Botticelli

The Birth of Venus
and detail on pages
58-59
Tempera on panel,
172.5 x 278.5 cm

Sandro Botticelli

Pallas and the Centaur
and detail on pages
26-27
Tempera on panel,
207 x 148 cm

Sandro Botticelli

Calumny
Tempera on panel,
62 x 91 cm

Filippino Lippi
(Prato 1457 - Florence
1504)

Adoration of the Magi
Tempera on panel,
258 x 243 cm

**Domenico Bigordi
called Ghirlandaio**
(Florence 1449 - 1494)

Adoration of the Magi
Tempera on panel,
diam. 172 cm

**Roger
van der Weyden**
(Tournai c. 1400 -
Brussels 1464)

*The Deposition
in the Tomb*, detail
Oil on panel,
110 x 96 cm

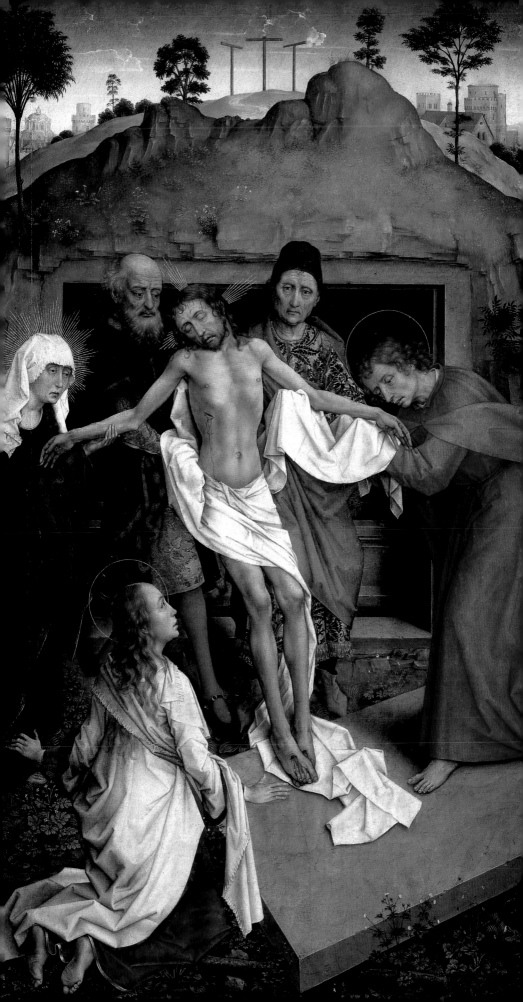

Hugo van der Goes
(Ghent c. 1440 -
Roode Kloster, Brussels
1482)

Portinari Triptych
Oil on panel,
253 x 586 cm (total)

Hans Memling
(Seligenstadt c. 1435 -
Bruges 1494)

Saint Benedict
Oil on panel,
45.5 x 34.5

Hans Memling

*Portrait of Benedetto
Portinari*
Oil on panel,
45 x 34 cm

Andrea di Cione called Verrocchio
(Florence 1435 - Venice 1488)
and **Leonardo da Vinci**
(Vinci 1452 - Amboise 1519)

The Baptism of Christ
Tempera on panel,
180 x 152 cm

Leonardo da Vinci

Annunciation and detail
on following pages
Tempera on panel,
98 x 217 cm

Leonardo da Vinci

Adoration of the Magi
Tempera mixed with oil
with parts in red and
greenish lacquer,
or white lead,
243 x 246 cm

**Pietro Vannucci
called Perugino**
(Città della Pieve
c. 1448 - Fontignano
1523)

*Madonna and Child
with Saints*
Tempera on panel,
178 x 164 cm

Perugino
Pietà
Tempera on panel,
168 x 176 cm

Perugino
*Portrait of Francesco
delle Opere*, detail
Tempera on panel,
52 x 44 cm

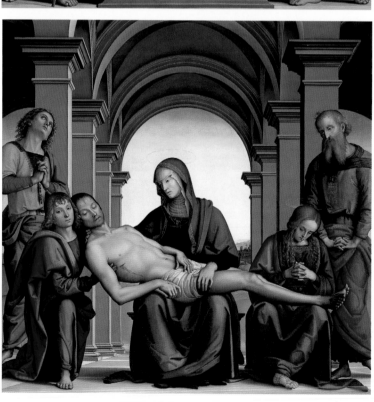

Luca Signorelli
(Cortona 1445/50 -
1523)

Holy Family
Tempera on panel,
diam. 124 cm

Luca Signorelli

*Madonna and Child
with Allegorical Figures*
Tempera on panel,
170 x 117.5 cm

Andrea Mantegna
(Isola di Carturo 1431 -
Mantua 1506)

*Portrait of Cardinal
Carlo de' Medici*, detail
Tempera on panel,
40.5 x 29.5 cm

Andrea Mantegna

Triptych with the
Epiphany, Circumcision
and *Ascension*
Tempera on panel,
77 x 75 cm (central
panel), 86 x 42.5
(side panels)

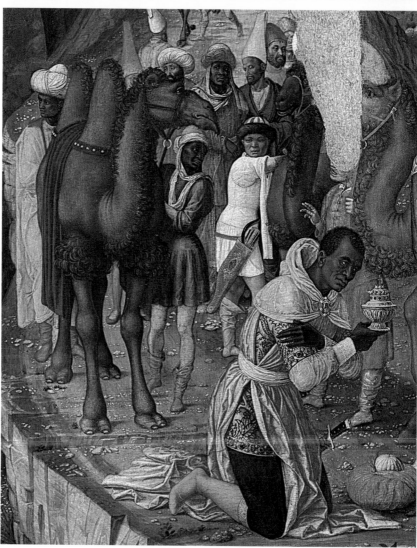

Among the paintings of the early 16th century, it is worth singling out the *Rescue of Andromeda* by Piero di Cosimo, a work characterized by an unusual fantastic dimension. The enigmatic *Allegory* by the Venetian Giovanni Bellini is rich in symbolic meaning. Also from the Veneto region are two small panels by Giorgione, *The Judgment of Solomon* and *The Trial of Moses*, and a vigorous *Warrior with Equerry*, attributed to the same artist. These are followed by a group of important works by German artists: Dürer, Altdorfer, Lucas Cranach the Elder and Hans Holbein the Younger.

But let us return to Florence, where the Renaissance had reached its peak with the presence of two artists like Michelangelo and Raphael. In the *Doni Tondo*, one of the works most emblematic of the gallery, Michelangelo paradoxically underlines his belief in the supremacy of sculpture over painting, proposing a plastic and anti-naturalistic vision that would later be reinterpreted and developed by the exponents of the Mannerist style. Raphael's Florentine period is represented by the *Madonna of the Goldfinch*, while the intense *Portrait of Leo X with Two Cardinals* belongs to the artist's full maturity, painted in Rome in the years 1517-18. Alongside these two main protagonists, other significant figures were active in Florence during this period, including Francesco Granacci, Franciabigio, Mariotto Albertinelli and Andrea del Sarto. But perhaps the two most interesting personalities are those of Pontormo and Rosso, the two principal exponents of the Mannerist movement, who took the lesson of Michelangelo to its extreme formal consequences. A contrast to this complex art was provided, several years later, by the polished but vigorous portraiture of Agnolo Bronzino, who painted the likenesses of the whole of the Medici family, as well as those of many Florentine aristocrats of the time.

Going back to the Veneto region, we encounter the great figure of Titian, who is represented in the Uffizi by several masterpieces, including the wonderful *Venus of Urbino*. Then there are, among others, works by Sebastiano del Piombo, Lorenzo Lotto, Veronese and Jacopo Tintoretto. The various Emilian artists of the period whose work is to be found in the museum include Parmigianino, with his famous *Madonna with the Long Neck*, and the Ferrarese Dosso Dossi.

Piero di Cosimo
(Florence 1461/62 -
1521)

*The Rescue of
Andromeda* and detail
on previous pages
Oil on panel,
70 x 123 cm

**Giovanni Bellini
called Giambellino**
(Venice 1425/30 -
1516)

Allegory
Oil on panel,
73 x 119 cm

Giorgione
(Castelfranco Veneto
c. 1477 - Venice 1510)

*The Judgment
of Solomon
The Trial of Moses*
Oil on panel,
89 x 72 cm each

Giorgione, attrib.
Warrior with Equerry
Oil on canvas,
90 x 73 cm

Albrecht Dürer
(Nuremberg
1471 - 1528)

Adoration of the Magi
Oil on panel,
99 x 113.5 cm

Albrecht Altdorfer
(Regensburg?
c. 1480 - 1538)

*The Departure
of Saint Florian*
Oil on panel,
81.4 x 67 cm

*The Martyrdom
of Saint Florian*
Oil on panel,
76.4 x 67.2 cm

**Hans Holbein
the Younger**
(Augsburg 1497/98 -
London 1543)

*Portrait of Sir Richard
Southwell*
Oil on panel,
47.5 x 38 cm

**Lucas Cranach
the Elder**
(Kronach 1472 -
Weimar 1553)

Adam and Eve
Oil on panel,
172 x 63 cm,
167 x 61 cm

**Michelangelo
Buonarroti**
(Caprese, Arezzo,
1475 - Rome 1564)

Holy Family
(*Doni Tondo*)
Tempera on panel,
diam. 120 cm

Raphael
(Urbino 1483 - Rome
1520)

*Madonna
of the Goldfinch*
Tempera on panel,
107 x 77 cm

Raphael

Portrait of Leo X
with Two Cardinals
Tempera on panel,
155.5 x 119.5 cm

**Antonio Allegri
called Correggio**
(Reggio Emilia 1489 -
1534)

Adoration of the Child
Oil on canvas,
81 x 77 cm

Francesco Granacci
(Florence 1477 - 1543)

*Joseph Presenting
His Father and Brother
to the Pharaoh*
Tempera on panel,
95 x 224 cm

**Francesco
di Cristofano
called Franciabigio**
(Florence 1484 - 1525)

Portrait of a Young Man
Oil on panel,
60 x 47 cm

**Andrea d'Agnolo
called Andrea
del Sarto**
(Florence 1486 - 1530)

*Portrait of Woman
Reading Petrarch*
Oil on panel,
87 x 69 cm

Andrea del Sarto

*Madonna
of the Harpies*
Oil on panel,
207 x 178 cm

Jacopo Carucci
called Pontormo
(Pontorme, Empoli
1494 - Florence 1556)

The Supper at Emmaus,
detail
Oil on canvas,
230 x 173 cm

Pontormo

Portrait of Cosimo
the Elder
Oil on panel,
86 x 65 cm

**Giovan Battista
di Jacopo called
Rosso Fiorentino**
(Florence 1494 -
Fontainebleau 1540)

*Madonna and Child
with Saints*
Oil on panel,
172 x 141 cm

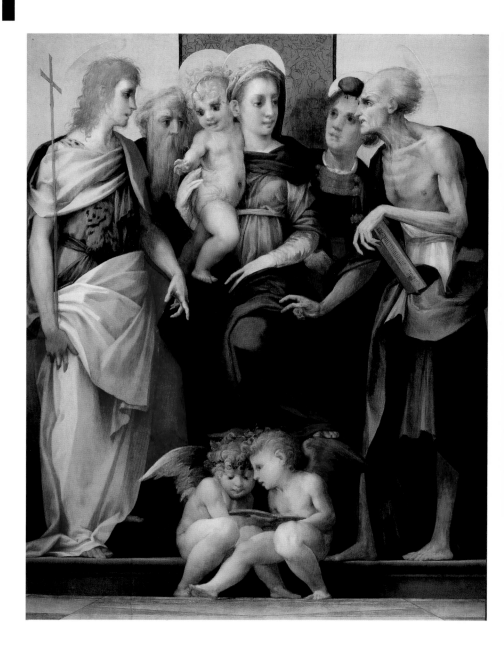

following pages:
Rosso Fiorentino

*Moses Defending the
Daughters of Jethro,*
detail
Oil on canvas,
160 x 117 cm

Agnolo di Cosimo called Agnolo Bronzino
(Florence 1503 - 1572)

Portrait of Eleonora of Toledo with Her Son Giovanni
Oil on panel,
115 x 96 cm

Agnolo Bronzino

Portrait of Bia de' Medici
Oil on panel,
63 x 48 cm

Agnolo Bronzino

Portrait of Man with a Lute
Oil on panel,
98 x 82.5 cm

Giorgio Vasari
(Arezzo 1511 - Florence 1574)

Portrait of Lorenzo the Magnificent
Oil on panel,
90 x 72 cm

Agnolo Bronzino

Portrait of Lucrezia Panciatichi, detail
Oil on panel,
104 x 84 cm

Titian
(Pieve di Cadore
c. 1488 - Venice 1576)

*Portrait of a Man,
"The Sick Man"*
Oil on canvas,
81 x 60 cm

**Jacopo Negretti
called Palma il Vecchio**
(Serina, Bergamo,
c. 1480 - Venice 1528)

Judith
Oil on panel,
90 x 71 cm

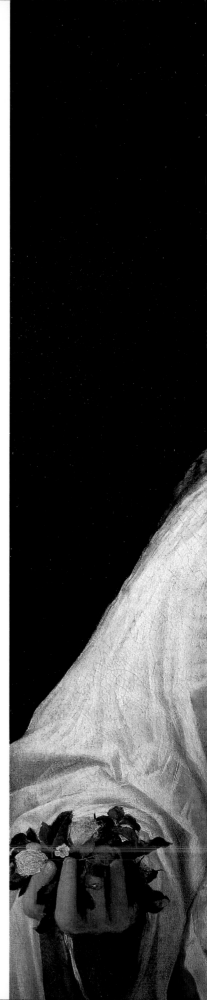

Titian

Flora
Oil on canvas,
79,7 x 63.5 cm

Titian

Venus of Urbino
Oil on canvas,
119 x 165 cm

**Sebastiano Luciani
called Sebastiano
del Piombo**
(Venezia c. 1485 -
Rome 1547)

Death of Adonis
Oil on canvas,
189 x 285 cm

Sebastiano del Piombo

Portrait of a Woman
Oil on panel,
68 x 55 cm

Francesco Mazzola called Parmigianino
(Parma 1503 - Casalmaggiore 1540)

Portrait of a Man
Oil on panel,
88 x 68.5 cm

Lorenzo Lotto
(Venice c. 1480 -
Loreto c. 1556)

Susanna and the Elders
Oil on panel,
66 x 50 cm

**Giovan Battista Luteri
called Dosso Dossi**
(Ferrara c. 1489 -
1542)

Witchcraft
Oil on canvas,
143 x 144 cm

Parmigianino
*Madonna with
the Long Neck*
Oil on panel,
219 x 135 cm

**School of
Fontainebleau**
(second half
of 16th century)

Two Women Bathing
Oil on panel,
129 x 97 cm

François Clouet
(Tours c. 1510 - Paris
1572)

King Francis I of France
Oil on panel,
27.5 x 22.5 cm

**Paolo Caliari
called Veronese**
(Verona 1528 - Venice
1588)

*Holy Family
with Saints Barbara
and John*
Oil on canvas,
86 x 122 cm

**Jacopo da Ponte
called Jacopo
Bassano**
(Bassano c. 1517 -
1592)

Two Dogs
Oil on canvas,
85 x 126 cm

**Giovanni Battista
Moroni**
(Albino 1529/30 -
Bergamo 1578)

*Portrait of Pietro
Secco Suardo*
Oil on canvas,
183 x 104 cm

Federico Barocci
(Urbino 1535 - 1612)

Madonna del Popolo,
detail
Oil on panel,
359 x 272 cm

Federico Barocci

*Portrait of Francesco
Maria II della Rovere*
Oil on canvas,
113 x 93 cm

Jacopo Robusti
called Tintoretto
(Venice 1518 - 1594)

Leda and the Swan
Oil on canvas,
162 x 218 cm

Tintoretto

Portrait of Jacopo
Sansovino
Oil on canvas,
70 x 65.5 cm

Tintoretto

Portrait of Man
with a Red Beard
Oil on canvas,
52.5 x 45.5 cm

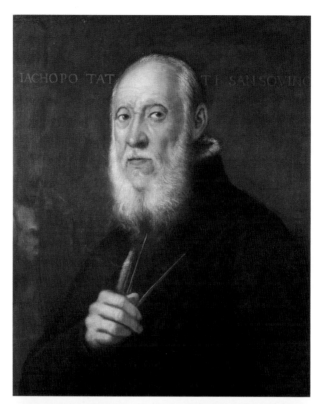

Domenikos Theotokópoulos called El Greco
(Candia 1541 - Toledo 1614)

Saints John the Evangelist and Francis
Oil on canvas, 110 x 86 cm

The focal point of 17th-century painting at the Uffizi is unquestionably Caravaggio, three of whose finest works can be seen in the gallery: the *Bacchus*, the *Medusa* and the *Sacrifice of Isaac*. In all three pictures the extraordinary revolutionary force of Caravaggio's painting is evident, in the powerful realism with which youths from the lower classes were called on to serve as models for pagan gods and figures from the scriptures, and in the unaccustomed and brutal use of light. A *Venus with Satyr and Cupids* by Annibale Carracci is full of references to the warm sensuality of Titian's art, while Artemisia Gentileschi's *Judith and Holofernes* is an example of the Caravaggesque current. But the names of many great masters of European painting also appear in the 17th-century section, commencing with Rubens. Here we reproduce the splendid *Portrait of Isabella Brandt,* a picture of the artist's wife, and a *Judith and Holofernes* that recent restoration has revealed to be the work of the Flemish painter. A follower of Rubens and great portraitist in the service of many European courts, Anthony van Dyck is represented here by two paintings depicting *Jean de Montfort* and *Charles V on Horseback*.

Rembrandt's predilection for the self-portrait, which he went on painting throughout his life, is well-known. Here we present two of the most famous of them: the first is an early one, while the second, in which the great Dutch artist has a somber and melancholic appearance, was executed at a much more advanced age. Among the other paintings from elsewhere in Europe, there are several landscapes. The *Port with the Villa Medici* by the celebrated French artist Claude Lorrain, painted for Cardinal Carlo de' Medici, places the real Medici residence in Rome in the completely imaginary setting of a port. More markedly Northern European in character are the pictures of two Dutch painters, *Landscape with Shepherds and Peasants* by Jacob van Ruisdael and a view of *The Groote Markt in Haarlem* by Gerrit Berckheyde.

Annibale Carracci
(Bologna 1560 - Rome
1609)

*Venus with Satyr
and Cupids*
Oil on canvas,
112 x 142 cm

Michelangelo Merisi called Caravaggio
(Caravaggio or Milan 1570/71 - Porto Ercole 1610)

Bacchus and detail on pages 124-125
Oil on canvas, 95 x 85 cm

Artemisia Gentileschi
(Rome 1593 - Naples
1652)

Judith and Holofernes
Oil on canvas,
199 x 162.5 cm

following pages:

Caravaggio

Sacrifice of Isaac,
detail
Oil on canvas,
104 x 135 cm

pages 132-133:

Caravaggio

Medusa, detail
Oil on canvas mounted
on panel, diam. 55 cm

Giovan Francesco Barbieri called Guercino
(Cento 1591 - Bologna 1660)

Country Concert
Oil on copper,
34 x 46 cm

Claude Gellée called Lorrain
(Chamagne, Nancy 1600 - Rome 1682)

Port with the Villa Medici
Oil on canvas,
102 x 133 cm

Peter Paul Rubens
(Siegen 1577 -
Antwerp 1640)

Judith and Holofernes
Oil on canvas,
113 x 89 cm

Peter Paul Rubens

*Portrait of Isabella
Brandt*, detail
Oil on panel,
86 x 62 cm

136

Anthony van Dyck
(Antwerp 1599 -
London 1641)

Charles V on Horseback
Oil on canvas,
191 x 123 cm

Anthony van Dyck

*Portrait of Jean
de Montfort*
Oil on canvas,
123 x 86 cm

Jacob Jordaens
(Antwerp 1593-1678)

Portrait of a Lady
Oil on canvas,
68 x 50 cm

**Rembrandt
Harmenszoon
van Rijn**
(Leiden 1606 -
Amsterdam 1669)

Self-Portrait as an Old Man
Oil on canvas,
74 x 55 cm

**Rembrandt
Harmenszoon
van Rijn**

*Self-Portrait as
a Young Man*, detail
Oil on canvas,
62.5 x 54 cm

Jacob van Ruisdael
(Haarlem 1628/29 -
Amsterdam? 1682)

*Landscape
with Shepherds
and Peasants*
Oil on canvas,
52 x 60 cm

Gabriel Metsu
(Leiden 1629 -
Amsterdam 1667)

A Lady and a Knight
Oil on panel,
66 x 50 cm

Gerrit Berckheyde
(Haarlem 1631/32 -
1664)

*The Groote Markt
in Haarlem*
Oil on canvas,
56 x 64 cm

We open the section of 18th-century works with a fine still life by the Dutch painter Rachel Ruysch, which unites the conventions of her country's long tradition in this genre with her own documentary and scientific interests.

The influence of Dutch and Flemish painting can also be discerned in the curious genre scene depicted in *The Flea* by Giuseppe Maria Crespi, a Bolognese artist who was active at the court of Prince Ferdinando de' Medici for several years. Originally on the ceiling of the Seminario Arcivescovile in Udine, the large canvas by Giambattista Tiepolo depicting the *Erection of a Statue in Honor of an Emperor* presents the typical characteristics of this painter's art, from the limpid luminosity of the backgrounds to the daring illusionistic inventions with which he constructed his own architectural compositions. Venetian *vedutismo* is represented by the paintings of two exceptional masters of the genre, Canaletto's *View of the Doge's Palace* and Francesco Guardi's *Seascape with Arch*. Another painting from Venice, but a genre scene this time, is *The Confession* by Pietro Longhi, extraordinary narrator of the everyday life of his city.

The genre painting of the 18th century found an original and poetic interpreter in the Frenchman Jean-Baptiste-Siméon Chardin. The Uffizi possesses a delightful pair of pictures by him, representing a *Girl with Racket and Shuttlecock* and a *Boy Playing Cards*.

In conclusion, several examples of 18th-century portraiture, very different from one another: the first, by the Genevan Jean-Étienne Liotard, depicts *Marie Adelaide of France* in a setting of a very intimate and private character, while in the second, the French painter François-Xavier Fabre portrays the poet *Vittorio Alfieri* in formal pose and dress. Finally, two masterpieces by Francisco Goya, in which we find the distinctive features of the painting of the great Spanish master, portray *The Countess of Chinchón Standing* and *Maria Teresa de Vallabriga on Horseback*.

Rachel Ruysch
(Amsterdam
1664 - 1750)

Fruit and Insects
Oil on panel,
44 x 60 cm

**Giovanni Antonio
Canal called
Canaletto**
(Venice 1697 - 1768)
*View of the Doge's
Palace*
Oil on canvas,
45 x 73 cm

Francesco Guardi
(Venice 1712 - 1793)
Seascape with Arch
Oil on canvas,
30 x 53 cm

Giambattista Tiepolo
(Venice 1696 - Madrid
1770)
*Erection of a Statue
in Honor of an Emperor*
Oil on canvas,
420 x 175 cm

Giuseppe Maria
Crespi
(Bologna 1665 - 1747)

The Flea
Oil on copper,
46.5 x 34 cm

Pietro Falca
called Pietro Longhi
(Venice 1702 - 1785)

The Confession
Oil on canvas,
61 x 49.5 cm

François-Xavier
Fabre
(Montpellier
1766 - 1837)

Portrait of
Vittorio Alfieri
Oil on canvas,
93 x 73 cm

Jean-Etienne Liotard
(Ginevra 1702 - 1789)

Marie Adelaide of France
and detail on pages
144-145
Oil on canvas,
50 x 56 cm

**Francisco de Goya
y Lucientes**
(Fuendetodos 1746 -
Bordeaux 1828)

*The Countess
of Chinchón*
Oil on canvas,
220 x 140 cm

**Francisco de Goya
y Lucientes**

*Maria Teresa
de Vallabriga
on Horseback*
Oil on canvas,
82.5 x 61.7 cm

Index of Artists

Opposite, Florentine school of the
late 16th century, grotesque decoration
of the ceiling of the first corridor.

The illustrations in this volume have been supplied
by the SCALA PICTURE LIBRARY,
the largest source of color transparencies and digital images
of the visual arts in the world.
The over 60,000 subjects visible at the site
www.scalarchives.it
can be accessed through computerized procedures
that permit easy and rapid picture searches of any complexity.

e-mail: archivio@scalagroup.com

Granphic Design and Editing: Studio Contri Toscano
Translation: Huw Evans
Photographs: SCALA Picture Library

The images from the SCALA Picture Library reproducing cultural assets
that belong to the Italian State are published with the permission
of the Ministry for Cultural Heritage and Activities

Printed by: D'Auria Industrie Grafiche S.p.A., Ascoli Piceno, 2004